Bibliographical Series
of Supplements to 'British Book News'
on Writers and Their Work

GENERAL EDITOR
Bonamy Dobrée

¶ CHRISTOPHER SMART was born on 11 April 1722 at Shipbourne, near Tunbridge, Kent. He died on 21 May 1771 in the rules of the King's Bench, London and was buried in St. Paul's Churchyard.

CHRISTOPHER SMART

from a portrait at Pembroke College, Cambridge,
reproduced by kind permission of the Master and Fellows

CHRISTOPHER SMART

by

GEOFFREY GRIGSON

PUBLISHED FOR
THE BRITISH COUNCIL
and the NATIONAL BOOK LEAGUE
by LONGMANS, GREEN & CO.

LONGMANS, GREEN & CO. LTD.
48 Grosvenor Street, London W.1
Thibault House, Thibault Square, Cape Town
605–611 Lonsdale Street, Melbourne C.1.

LONGMANS, GREEN & CO. INC.
119 West 40th Street, New York 18

LONGMANS, GREEN & CO.
20 Cranfield Road, Toronto 16

ORIENT LONGMANS PRIVATE LTD.
Calcutta   Bombay   Madras
Delhi   Hydrabad   Dacca

First Published in 1961
© Geoffrey Grigson 1961

Printed in Great Britain by
F. Mildner & Sons, London, E.C.1

CHRISTOPHER SMART

I

To BE mad or to be under the influence of opium are strange conditions. The writing of poems is a strange activity, and poets who have written in madness or when opium has in some way altered the activity of their minds, appear doubly, 'romantically', strange or mysterious. So we have our vision of Coleridge interrupted, after his opium sleep, upon the writing of *Kubla Khan;* of Crabbe pierced, in his opium nightmares, by the keen streamers of the Northern Lights, of De Quincey (a poet in prose) transfixed by minarets; of Hölderlin, mad in his tower above the still Neckar; of Collins howling in Chichester Cathedral; of Blake observing angels or the ghost of a flea; of John Clare lost in a contemplation of the sun, or declaring that the vowels had been picked out through his ears; and of Christopher Smart, praying naked in the rain, or inscribing (a less improbable tale than some commentators have maintained) stanzas of his *A Song to David*, with a key, on the wainscot of his madhouse room. Whether cause and consequence are allied quite in the way we imagine is another matter; but there is no doubt of the frequent intimacy of the strange condition and the strange activity. It is certainly true that in Smart's case the one important activity, the poems, cannot be entirely considered without the other. Either madness, in this case, or the attendant circumstances of confinement, with its release from drunkenness, distraction, responsibility, and other pressures, including the pressure of current intellectual fashion, enabled Smart to concentrate his mind for a while in trance-like states of pure consciousness. He was able to release, combine, and shape the important elements of his life experience, intellectual and sensual.

II

A first fact of Christopher Smart's poetry is confirmed by the prologue of his life—the fact of a contradiction in himself, psychologically and intellectually, and between himself —between his own psychological constitution—and the particular, and rather cautious, balance of mind commonly favoured or approved in his century. Smart was born in 1722 at Shipbourne on the edge of the Kentish Weald. There he lived for his first years, his father steward to the Vanes (he was perhaps named Christopher after Sir Christopher Vane, the first Lord Barnard who died at Fairlawn the year after his birth), himself free of his parents' garden, of the Vanes' estate of Fairlawn, and of an exceedingly rich and speckled and variegated countryside, full of flowers and fruit, wooded, cultivated, watered, valley-divided, part wild, part subdued and ordered. He was schooled a few miles away at Maidstone, on the slow silvered stream of the Medway. He had been premature at birth, and he remained delicate as a child (and later), an only son among sisters, who was dosed with cordials, which may have conditioned him, it was believed in his family, to his later drunkenness. In addition he was small, below normal height; as small a creature, in later manhood, as John Clare or De Quincey. His father died when this peculiar child was eleven years old, whereupon the family left Kent for the native Durham of the Smarts. This was a deprivation; but in the north Christopher Smart also had—and greatly enjoyed, one may think—the freedom of a different neighbourhood, no less remarkable than the one he had left, the florescent limestone country of the upland parish of Staindrop, the country of the Teesdale estates of Raby Castle, the headquarters of the noble family which had employed his father in Kent. In his Durham years he appears to have undergone an experience with its parallel in the lives of De Quincey, Hölderlin and John Clare—a second experience of deprivation. He fell in love, it seems, with

Anne Vane, daughter of his patron Lord Barnard, and attempted a childish elopement with her. The suggestion that she was afterwards the ideal object of his constancy (though he set himself at other women, married, and had children), would fit in well with Smart's mental and imaginative history. He refers to Anne Vane several times at any rate in the half-mad antiphony of his *Jubilate Agno*. She was Hope (having become Lady Anne Hope):

> For X is hope—consisting of two check G—God be gracious to Anne Hope,

she was Constancy, and he had visions of her:

> Let Constant, house of Constant rejoice with the Musk-Goat— I bless God for two visions of Anne Hope's being in charity with me,

and he appears once to remember her with a special liveliness and poignancy:

> For the blessing of God upon purity is in the Virgin's blushes
> For the blessing of God in colour is on him that keeps his virgin.
> For I saw a blush in Staindrop Church, which was of God's own colouring.
> For it was the benevolence of a virgin shewn to me before the whole congregation.

In *Jubilate Agno* Smart was also to remember the delight of living at Shipbourne, calling for a blessing on the Fairlawn estate:

> Let Shechem of Manasseh rejoice with the Green Worm whose livery is of the field.
> . . . .
> For I bless God in SHIPBOURNE FAIRLAWN the meadows the brooks and the hills.

It was his schooling, and his university in particular, which overlaid at first this prologue of his being. Emotionally he was deeply excited, at times possessed, by the splendours

and sparklings of nature. This excitement could be justified
by a simple *Te Deum laudamus*, a *Benedicite, omnia opera;*
but even then it tended towards a heat of imagination
beyond reason, which this fellow of his college (as he became
in 1745), this classical scholar, could not approve. It invited
metaphysical speculation, on the side of 'enthusiasm', which
he would be chary of accepting. His madness overwhelmed
him first in 1756, in his early thirties. Whether written in
his Cambridge or his London years, as a fellow of Pembroke
Hall or as a publisher's hack, his poems up to that time had
been mostly of the kind which critics and readers looked
for. In songs 'sweetly elegant and pretty', in facetious
verses, even in his pieces of solemn rhetoric, and more
complex organisation, and more imaginative tone, he was
a conformist. He could translate a snowball into a snowy
orb—'When, wanton fair, the snowy orb you throw',
or with a more solemn triteness he could instruct the
reader in an *Ode on Saint Cecilia's Day* that the saint was a
'matchless Dame'. Yet such conventionalism was now and
then breached or contradicted. Sometimes his later width,
depth and sparkle of a baroque vision flickers into view
and disappears:

> As some vast vista, whose extent
> Scarce bounded by the firmament
>   From whence it's sweep begun;
> Above, beneath, in every place,
> Mark'd with some grand distinguish'd grace,
>   Ends with the golden sun:
>   [To the King]

Sometimes a sparkling item of the vision of earth finds the
right crystallization in a poem otherwise awkward:

> Their scythes upon the adverse bank
>   Glitter 'mongst th' entangled trees,
> Where the hazles form a rank,
>   And court'sy to the courting breeze.
>   [A Noon-Piece]

Or a spontaneous recognition of the moment overcomes conventional artifice, Smart, for example, ending a poem which he wrote in 1752 in the garden of a Quaker friend, in this way:

> Where Light and Shade in varied Scenes display
> A Contrast sweet, like friendly *yea* and *nay*.
> My Hand, the Secretary of my Mind,
> Left thee these Lines upon the *poplar's* Rind.
>   [To my Worthy Friend Mr. T. B.]

Readers excited by the summit of Smart's baroque peculiarity and grandeur of adoration are apt to turn to his earliest sustained poem *The Hop-Garden*, published in 1752, but evidently written when he was a boy, and then to turn away from it disappointed. It is certainly an exercise —a very odd one at times, as when beautiful Dorinda starts and frowns with indignation at finding in the dried foreign fruit for the Christmas pudding a negro's toe-nail— in that eighteenth century Miltonism which was reserved for celebrating pastoral pursuits or topographical sublimities:

> Whether you shiver in the marshy Weald,
> Egregious shepherds of unnumber'd flocks,
>   . . . or in fair Madum's vale
> Imparadis'd, blest denizens, ye dwell;
> Or Dorovernia's awful tow'rs ye love:
> Or plough Tunbridgia's salutiferous hills
> Industrious, and with draughts chalybiate heal'd,
> Confess divine Hygeia's blissful seat.

But examine *The Hop-Garden* with a retrospective sympathy, and there will be found in it a number of those first sensory impacts, those metallic illuminations, which were to obsess Smart years later in the creative excess of his vision. Silver surfaces (of the Medway) reflect:

> Now bloom the florid hops, and in the stream
> Shine in their floating silver . . .

Silvery fish, at any rate 'silver bleak, and prickly pearch', glide through the river; Northern Lights sparkle; Chanticleer is the bird which 'explodes the night'; green leaves suggest the music of Orpheus, who is to become the great psalmist of *A Song to David;* and Shipbourne, or the Fairlawn estate in Shipbourne parish, suggests already to Smart that recurrent image, of the interaction of the wild and the composed, of nature and art, of imagination and reason, of the hard gem of an uncultivated flower and the scythe-shaven grass, which was to become a structural integrator of Smart's vision:

> Next Shipbourne, tho' her precincts are confin'd
> To narrow limits, yet can show a train
> Of village beauties, pastorally sweet,
> And rurally magnificent. Here Fairlawn
> Opes her delightful prospects; dear Fairlawn
> There, where at once at variance and agreed,
> Nature and art hold dalliance. There where rills
> Kiss the green drooping herbage, there where trees
> The tall trees tremble at th'approach of heav'n,
> And bow their salutation to the sun,
> Who fosters all their foliage—These are thine,
> Yes, little Shipbourne, boast that these are thine—
> And if—but oh!—and if 'tis no disgrace,
> The birth of him who now records thy praise.

III

The Hop-Garden is the adolescent's tribute to the loved place. The university, a master's degree, a fellowship, wider reading and enquiry supervene; and against *The Hop-Garden* should be set the five blank verse essays which won Smart the Seatonian Prize in 1750, 1751, 1752, 1754 and again in 1756. Smart's ultimate grandiloquence crystallizes in a conjunction of the natural and the grandly visioned, the curiously observed and the grandly imagined, a baroque vision, as if a soaring, crowded, sparkling, coloured, active, three dimensional interior, shall I say, of an eighteenth century German baroque church by the Brothers Adam or Dominikus Zimmerman, full of flowers, fruits, figures, emblems, immediacies and infinities, and scraps of reflective surface, had been condensed and simplified in Protestant terms. This baroque vision of Smart's was given its trial run in the Seatonian poems. The prize, established under the Will of the Cambridge divine and hymnologist Thomas Seaton, went each year to the best poem celebrating a perfection or an attribute of the Supreme Being. It was in 1749 that Smart had left Cambridge for London, a victim of drink and debt, a man whose clowning and inconsequential gaiety were at some odds with his inner nature, a recognized scholar already looked upon as a weakling and an eccentric on the way either to the debtor's prison or the madhouse. So his prize poems were all of them written in his new and even less satisfactory life as a London journalist. Year by year, they at least kept him a footing in the university world from which he was now an exile. They were popular. They were also a fervent counterbalance to his daily writings of squibs and songs and occasional pieces, a recurrent reversion to his graver interests, emotionally and intellectually. In the second of these poems, *On the Immensity of the Supreme Being* (1751), Smart already looks on himself, publisher's creature or no, as a psalmist in the succession of David, the poem abruptly beginning:

> Once more I dare to raise the sounding string,
> *The poet of my God*—Awake my glory,
> Awake my lute and harp—my self shall wake,
> Soon as the stately night-exploding bird
> In lively lay sings welcome to the dawn.

It is David again who opens the poem *On the Power of the Supreme Being* (1754); and, with still more emphasis and effect, this hero of Smart's opens the last of these prize poems, *On the Goodness of the Supreme Being* (1756), in

which, classical scholar as well as Christian exegete, Smart
adopts an identification of David of the Hebrews and
Orpheus of the pagans, the two sweetest singers and
musicians:

> Orpheus, for so the Gentiles call'd thy name,
> Israel's sweet psalmist, who alone could wake
> The' inanimate to motion; who alone
> The joyful hillocks, the applauding rocks,
> And floods with musical persuasion drew;
> Thou, who to hail and snow gav'st voice and sound,
> And mad'st the mute melodious!— . . .
>   . . . in this breast
> Some portion of thy genuine spirit breathe,
> And lift me from myself.

In these poems, these annual liftings of Smart from the
Grub Street of London, he not only combined detail of
earth and the choir of heaven, he combined his experience
of a limited and a wider nature, observation with reading,
his own eye with the eye of travellers, naturalists, and
scientists,—the known to him with the imagined by him.
The Supreme Being, eternal, immense, omniscient, power-
ful, and good. His seraphim and His cherubim, are conjunct
in the poems with—for example—astronomical phenomena,
sun, moon, comets, stars, planets, Saturn and his ring.
Meteorological or optical concerns, refraction, colours,
rainbow, thunder, hurricane, join heaven to earth; on
earth the 'central magnet', and ores, fossils, crystals, gems
sparkling in the deep mines of Gani, Roalconda, Peru,
Ceylon, the Pyrenees, diamond, jasper, garnet, moss-agate
presenting its curious pictures, and ruby:

> Where the rich ruby . . .
>   . . . sparkles ev'n like Sirius
> And blushes into flames

—all these encounter corals, pearls and amber observed in
sea-depths; and these hard brilliants are in turn associated
with other activities, other strange or brilliant items of the

created earth: with earthquakes and eruptions and molten fire; with cataracts, caves, lakes, mountains; with beasts: lion, elephant, Leviathan, African camels (carrying ingots of gold); with insects: ant, glow-worm, bee; with birds: woodland warblers, woodlark, redbreast, linnet, ring-dove, jay, nightingale, peacock, raven; with flowers: tulip, auricula, peach blossom, lilies, roses, hawthorn, pansies, deadly nightshade, dock, hemlock; with fruit: pomegranate, pineapple, cherry, plum; and these again with the spices and gums of Arabia; all in a geographical range outwards to the Antarctic. The catalogue is curious, though hardly exceptional, scientifically, in view of Smart's known and probable reading, or poetically, in its glitter and variety, if we think of poets from Marvell and Milton and Waller to Pope himself, whom Smart greatly admired. Also images and glittering objects in array are one thing, poetry is another. For the most part these Seatonian poems by Smart indicate, but do not involve, do not create and proffer. They indicate a supposed creation, indicate the God-made, God-declaring, divinely good universe which Smart observes, but they do not condense it and transform it into compelling poetry. The rhetoric, like the rhythm, is still conventional (even at times absurd, as, for instance, when Smart writes of 'the domestic animal'—scilicet 'dog'—who 'from th' emetic herbage works his cure'), and is little shaped by that 'impression', verbal and rhythmical and constructive, which was soon to be the mark of Christopher Smart in his poems of madness or at least confinement. So the interest is prospective. These Seatonian exercises declare his bent, in the intervals between the writing of facetiae and empty lyrics, or in the intervals of being carried home dead drunk from the London beer-houses. They exhibit a ranging, but not yet a compelled constructive sensuality, a quadripartite openness to sight, sound, touch, scent:

> . . . sweeter than the breath of May
> Caught from the nectarine's blossom

—yet not much more than the spectator, facing the wonders of creation, reciting his own Benedicite.

The mix is made, the thermometer has still to rise, the new substance has still to combine and emerge.

In part, the somewhat conventional ardour of the religious spectator in these poems may have been due to Smart's own chariness of 'enthusiasm', a taint of which, or of anything at all intellectually or physico-theologically unusual, it would hardly have been tactful or proper to display on the surface, at any rate of poems entered in a university religious competition, which might each of them win him a prize of a £30 he very much needed. Yet chary or cautious, Smart was not ill-informed in natural philosophy as well as the mere natural history of his day. There is particular evidence of that in the curious jottings of *Jubilate Agno*. There is a poem, too, which he wrote in 1751 about one of the women he admired, in which Smart seems to make fun of himself or his own more phlegmatically inquisitive moments:

> Pedants of dull phlegmatic Turns
> Whose Pulse not beats, whose Blood not burns,
>   Read *Malebranche*, *Boyle*, and *Marriot*;
> I scorn their Philosophic Strife,
> And study Nature from the Life,
>   (Where most she shines) in *Harriote*.

He had looked into the physico-theologians, into Malebranche more or less pantheistic and tainted with enthusiasm, into Boyle, and no doubt into the *Essais de physique* of Edmé Marriotte, whose name gave him so convenient a crambo rhyme for the girl; and it has been plausibly argued that he went further (in the London years of his intermittent madness after 1756?) by accepting at last a Berkeleyan attitude, that nature, more than declaring the glory of God to the passive spectator in a direct psalmody, is joined to ourselves in our direct active perception, in which it exists concretely and brilliantly, and as a portion of divine language.

Such an acceptance, still rational, and avoiding 'enthusiasm' or pantheism, would help to explain the difference between the Seatonian poems, and the clipped, concrete, brilliant, eloquence of *A Song to David*, which Smart, student perhaps of Bishop Berkeley as of King David and the Three Children in the burning, fiery furnace, was to achieve at some time within the next seven years of intermittent mental illness.

IV

The seven dubious and anxious years lasted from 1756 to 1763. But neither the exact time-table of these years, nor the exact nature of Smart's madness are known. That he was ill in mind in 1755 or 1756, before being shut away, is certain from the *Hymn to the Supreme Being* (*on recovery from a dangerous fit of illness*), which he published in 1756, a stronger poem more directly, verbally, rhythmically in key with his emotion than any he had yet written. He suffered from "horrible despair", reason left him "and sense was lost in terror or in trance". But he recovered:

> My feeble feet refus'd my body's weight,
>   Nor wou'd my eyes admit the glorious light,
> My nerves convuls'd shook fearful of their fate,
>   My mind lay open to the powers of night.
> He pitying did a second birth bestow
> A birth of joy—not like the first of tears and woe.
>
> Ye strengthen'd feet, forth to his altar move;
>   Quicken, ye new-strung nerves, th' enraptur'd lyre;
> Ye heav'n-directed eyes, o'erflow with love;
>   Glow, glow, my soul, with pure seraphic fire;
> Deeds, thoughts, and words no more his mandates break,
> But to his endless glory work, conceive, and speak.

What is certain is that the new birth, new joy, was to be subject to ups and downs, or ups and outs. Twenty years after Smart's death, his nephew wrote that he had suffered from 'temporary alienations of mind; which at last were attended with paroxysms so violent and continued as to render confinement necessary'. The violence seems to have come upon him before 1756 was out, and the probable time-table was this, that later in 1756 he was first confined, according to the usual custom of the century, in private lodgings; that, not improving, he was transferred in the spring to the London madhouse of St. Luke's Hospital, where (it is certain) he lived for a year, from May 1757 to May 1758, when he was discharged as uncured. For a while he may now have been in private lodgings again or with his family. Evidently he became much worse in 1759. Garrick the actor gave a benefit performance for him in February, as if to raise money for a new confinement or new lodgings; and his friends wrote poems for the occasion in language suggesting that all was now over with Smart as a poet and a man. On or soon after 13 August he was shut up once more—probably in Bedlam (and possibly after an especially mad-seeming bout of praising God):

> For I bless the thirteenth of August, in which I had the grace to obey the voice of Christ in my conscience.

> For I bless the thirteenth of August, in which I was willing to run all hazards for the sake of the name of the Lord.

> For I bless the thirteenth of August, in which I was willing to be called a fool for the sake of Christ.

—and so he continued until he faced the world again in the New Year of 1763.

How mad was he? Not mad enough at any rate to be unable, even if intermittently, to read, meditate, feel, and write. His sanity ebbed and returned. With violence (which lasted for a while at any rate) he mixed a religious mania, both praying and praising as a new psalmist '*The Poet of my God*', and praying desperately, one may think, against the state he was in. He prayed and praised in public, as we know from the famous recollection which Boswell recorded from Dr. Johnson's talk in 1763 (the year in which Smart was out and about again). 'Madness frequently discovers itself merely by unnecessary deviation fron the usual modes of the world', said Johnson or Johnson-Boswell, who may not have known the full facts. 'My poor friend Smart shewed the disturbance of his mind, by falling upon his knees, and saying his prayers in the streets, or in any other unusual place.' And Boswell also recorded that earlier conversation between Johnson and Dr. Burney the musician, in which Johnson so memorably said: 'He insisted on people praying with him; and I'd as lief pray with Kit Smart as any one else. Another charge was, that he did not love clean linen; and I have no passion for it.'

A small, plump, dirtily-dressed man sonorously praying and praising in public—praying, we know from his *Jubilate Agno*, in St James's Park and in the Mall, trying to make others pray with him, and causing offence:

> Let Shobi rejoice with the Kastrel blessed be the name JESUS in falconry and in the MALL.

> For I blessed God in St James's Park till I routed all the company.

> Let Elkanah rejoice with Cymindis the Lord illuminate us against the powers of darkness.

> For the officers of the peace are at variance with me and the watch-man smites me with his staff.

—praying sometimes naked and in the rain for the sake of an extra purity:

> For to worship naked in the Rain is the bravest thing for the refreshing and purifying the body

—or praying on the flat leads of a neat porticoed common-sensible eighteenth century house:

> For a man should put no obstacle between his head and the blessing of Almighty God . . .

> For the ceiling of the house is an obstacle and therefore we pray on the house-top.

He not only prayed on his knees in public, literally following, it has been said, St Paul's injunction to the Thessalonians:

> Rejoice evermore.
> Pray without ceasing
> In everything give thanks . . .
> Quench not the Spirit
> Despise not prophesyings.
>   (*I Thessalonians*, 5,)

He also composed particular passages of his poems on his knees, that posture which he held to be 'a way to the terrestrial Paradise':

> For the method of philosophizing is in a posture of Adoration.

What were the conditions of his madness, or his confinement? In its ebb and swell he certainly felt humiliated and resentful, at first scrutinizing the visitors who came to the raree show of the madhouse, for someone to save him:

> For they pass by me in their tour, and the good Samaritan is not yet come.

at first objecting to the visitors' comments:

> For Silly fellow! Silly fellow! is against me and belongeth neither to me nor my family.

If he was violent at times (as when he instructed Andrew to 'rejoice with the Whale, who is arrayd in beauteous blue & is a combination of bulk and activity', because 'they work me with their harping-irons, which is a barbarous instrument, because I am no more unguarded than the others'), he would have known the chains and straw perhaps in a safety cell or dungeon. Somewhile after that entry on the harping irons, he wrote down, as though restored from such a cell to daylight:

> Let Sadoc rejoice with the Bleak, who playeth upon the surface in the Sun.

> For I bless God that I am not in a dungeon, but am allowed the light of the Sun.

It is on record that, being both a wit and a scholar, he was 'visited as such while under confinement.' After a while he grew fat as if more contented, and he dug in the garden, according to Boswell's *Life of Johnson:*

> BURNEY: 'How does poor Smart do, Sir; is he likely to recover?' JOHNSON: 'It seems as if his mind had ceased to struggle with the disease; for he grows fat upon it.' BURNEY: 'Perhaps, Sir, that may be from want of exercise.' JOHNSON: 'No, Sir; he has partly as much exercise as he used to have, for he digs in the garden.'

Flowers were the consequence of his asylum gardening, 'the Lord succeed my pink borders' Smart says in the *Jubilate*. These details are picked out and emphasized for a good reason; they relate (though the reference to the pink borders—and probably the digging and the fatness—dates from 1762) to the asylum months, in which it is most likely—and I think certain, on the evidence which has been advanced—that Smart wrote some of the *Hymns*, finished his *Psalms*, and wrote or finished, above all, *A Song to David*, the most sharply fused and greatest of all his poems, as well as writing the first three of the surviving fragments of *Jubilate Agno*, that strange antiphony which is half poem, half a species of journal.

Correspondence of topic and image and word suggest that some of the finest of the *Hymns* and the *Psalms* and *A Song to David* were written more or less concurrently with these early fragments of the *Jubilate*, which can be dated from the summer of 1759 to the summer of 1760. 'For the nightly Visitor' [the owl] 'is at the window of the impenitent, while I sing a psalm of my own composing' wrote Smart before the fateful 13 August, 1759. He seems to have been at work on the *Song;* and a little later, still before his last confinement, he adds: 'For I pray the Lord Jesus to translate my MAGNIFICAT into verse and represent it'.[1] Perhaps Bedlam or no, he had finished at any rate the Adoration stanzas by that time, early in 1760, when he wrote down that by the grace of God he was 'the Reviver of ADORATION amongst ENGLISH-MEN'.

V

It seems to me a fair, indeed inevitable conclusion that the 'matchless deed', which has been 'atchiev'd, DETERMINED, DARED, and DONE', as Smart so victoriously celebrates it in the last two lines of *A Song to David*, is capable of a tripartite explanation. Christ, David's 'son', as he explains himself, has brought salvation down; David, 'the best poet who ever lived', has achieved his psalmody; Christopher Smart, too, has achieved, has determined,

---

[1] Like Yeats setting out a preliminary in prose which he then worked into a poem, does this mean that Smart first wrote out prose preliminary to the *A Song of David*, in something of the style of the entries in *Jubilate Agno?*

dared, and finished, his own translation or version of those *Psalms*. It is true that the brief *Song* was not published until 1763, after Smart's release from the asylum, and that the lengthy *A Translation of the Psalms of David* into *Hymns and Spiritual Songs for the Fasts and Festivals of the Church of England* was published later still, in 1765. It is also true that in *Jubilate Agno*, in December and January 1763, towards the time of his release, he first asks, 'The Lord help on with the hymns', and then asks that the Lord should 'forward my translation of the psalms this year'. But this does not mean (I think) that the Lord should encourage a work still in progress, but that he should forward its publication. He also says 'I pray for a musician or musicians to set the new psalms' and 'I pray God bless all my Subscribers' (since the *Psalms and Hymns* were to be published by subscription), clearly speaking of something finished. The supposition that best fits the evidence, including the evidence inside the actual poems, is that he had completed the *Psalms*, at any rate a first draft of them all, by some date in 1759, whereupon he composed his own song of gratitude. In some of the *Psalms* it has been noticed that Smart unquestionably refers to himself as the inmate of an asylum, in Psalm XXXI for example:

> My name was nam'd as a reproof,
>   That neither friend nor foes,
> Nor neighbours came beneath my roof,
> And my companions kept aloof,
>   As other company they chose.

> The world have all my deeds forgot,
>   And I am in the place
> Of one, whose memory is not,
> Whose body damps sepulchral rot

(the last line suggests a damp punishment cell), or in Psalm XXXV:

'All that we surmise has follow'd,'
   Let them not with triumph boast,
'His remains the gulph has swallowed,
   He has given up the ghost.' [1]

Make them blush with shame ingenuous,
   Which at my distress rejoice;
Who against the truth are strenuous,
   Give them grace to hear her voice.

Let them say, which like the measure,
   That in charity I deal;
Blessed be the Lord, whose pleasure
   Is his servant's bliss to seal.

As for me in heavenly phrases
   I will harmonize my tongue,
Day by day Jehovah's praises
   Shall in sweeter notes be sung.

Having sung the last of the sweeter notes (whatever revision came later) somewhere about August or autumn of 1759, having come to the last Hosanna of David's psalms, at any rate in the first draft, what could have been more appropriate than to contrive now the psalm of his own composing, to translate his own Magnificat into verse, in the form and superb shape of that poem which Smart described afterwards as having been 'composed in a Spirit of affection and thankfulness to the great Author of the

---

[1] He perhaps refers to the rather sepulchral commendations which his friends had written at the time of Garrick's performance on his behalf a few months back in February. William Woty, for one, had described him as an 'unhappy bard' whose celestial harp was broken, 'affecting emblem of its master's fate'.

   Ah me! no more, I fear, its tuneful strings,
     Touch'd by his hand, will praise the *King of Kings*.
Through his life Smart must have heard much of the kind of talk which prophesied jail or madness for him. Gray the poet, as long back as 1747, had written to Warton the poet of Smart's vanity and lying and debts, all of which 'must come to a Jayl or Bedlam, and not without any help, almost without pity . . .'

Book of Gratitude, which is the *Psalms*, of DAVID the King', and which he prefaced on the title-page with David's words (2 Sam. xxiii, 2), 'The SPIRIT OF THE LORD spake by Me, and HIS WORD was in my Tongue'! In some degree his affection for David was increased by the thought of that 'serene suspence' in which David's singing had held 'The frantic throes of Saul'. As David for Saul, so David for Smart:

> His muse, bright angel of his verse,
> Gives balm for all the thorns that pierce,
>   For all the pangs that rage;
>   (*A Song to David*, Stanza XVII)

Incidentally, restoring *A Song to David* to 1759, or between 1759 and the early months of 1760, may also restore credibility to the story of the *Song*, the key and wainscot, which has always seemed to me both too vivid and too early (it occurs in the *Monthly Review* for April 1763, in a review of *A Song to David*) to be an invention. In August 1759, if the interpretation is correct, Smart had already begun the *Song*, a little mentally deranged, it may be, but at home or in private confinement. The thirteenth of August then introduced him into Bedlam or some other madhouse. It was soon after 31 August that he called upon Andrew to 'rejoice with the Whale, who is array'd in beauteous blue & is a combination of bulk & activity', because *they* were working him with their harping-irons, as if he were becoming violent, or was appearing violent or in some quieter way specially obnoxious to his keepers. Some time later he blesses God for not being in a dungeon, as if he had been released from punishment in a dark or dim room, or cell underground, such as the one in which he suffered those 'damps sepulchral' of his Psalm XXXI. The special confinement would have taken place while he was still at work on the precise incandescent architecture of the *Song*, and he may well for part of his time in that cell have been 'denied the use of pen, ink and paper', and have hammered out new stanzas of the *Song* in his head, which he was 'obliged to indent with one end of a key, upon the wainscot'.[1]

VI

To return for a moment to Smart's translation or version or adaptation, which is the better way of describing it, of the *Psalms*, it had been meditated no doubt for a long while. It is in line with the praise of David reiterated in his Seatonian poems; and was perhaps begun,—so at any rate the style suggests—after that recovery from the first recorded mental attack in 1755 or 1756, which had occasioned the *Hymn to the Supreme Being*, in that state of recovered reason and consequent exultation, of which he wrote:

> Brisk leaps the heart, the mind's at large once more,
> To love, to praise, to bless, to wonder and adore.

In the small print of the Muses' Library edition of Smart's poems, the *Psalms*, even without the supplementary *Hymns and Spiritual Songs*, fill more than 400 pages; and it is reasonable to think that Smart wrote such a bulk of verse in the lucid, or lucid enough, intervals of his mad years, (the portion of them between 1756 and 1759) when he was relieved, most of the while, from the nag of his debts and his normal responsibilities and employment. There is no reason to think that he must rigorously have followed the biblical order as he made his adaptations. Psalm XXXI, for instance, in which he refers to his asylum and which also contains the first weak version of the 'bastion's mole'

---

[1] *The Monthly Review* (1763).

of the 76th stanza of *A Song to David*, must have been written after many of the Psalms which follow. The very first of them, one may note, is written in the same stanza as *A Song to David*, and exhibits that alliterative tripartite summing of a final line to a stanza, *His bud, his bloom, and fruit*, which marks the *Song*, and which had appeared already in the *Hymn to the Supreme Being*. Now and again the Psalms show little of the ultimate stamp and virtuosity:

> Praise him, cherubic flights,
> And ye seraphic fires,
> Angelical delights
>   With voices, lutes and lyres;
> And vie who shall extol him most,
> Ye blest innumerable host!
>
> Praise him, thou source of heat,
>   Great ruler of the day,
> And thou serenely sweet,
>   O moon, his praise display;
> Praise him ye glorious lights that are,
> The planet and the sparkling star.

Again and again lines out of the *Psalms* are re-used or adapted to new use in the *Song*.

Yet it must be admitted that the *Psalms*, for all the amount of interpolation, for all their occasional force, and their scraps of felicity:

> The chearful trumpet sound,
> And let the horns be wound,
>   To yield thro' twisted brass their tone;

roll a little tediously along. By the time the great labour was dared and done Smart was at any rate expert in the stanza of *A Song to David*; he had employed it in some thirty of the Psalms, and the shape and sounds and rhythms of it must have been insistent in his mind. In the *Song*, his own *Magnificat*, the psalm of his own composing, the thanksgiving for his completed version of these *Psalms of David*, he was at last free altogether of any original; free to combine and condense a lifetime of sensory impact, of a select choice of recollections, of wonders glanced at in the Seatonian poems, noted loosely in the *Psalms*, more immediately in the antiphonal jottings of *Jubilate Agno* and (a few) in some of the earlier of the *Hymns and Spiritual Songs*. Now and again an image in the *Song* can be traced far back into his mental life:

> And, by the coasting reader spied,
> The silverlings and crusions glide
> For ADORATION gilt.

Silverlings are presumably roach, the crusion (properly Crucian or Crusian) is a fish of the carp family, yellow (i.e. gilt), introduced from Asia to continental Europe, and thence to England, where it was often put into ponds in the 18th century. *Jubilate Agno* shows that, in autumn 1759, in his madhouse, Smart had been recalling the fishponds and the fish of that Fairlawn where he had spent his childhood:

> Let Mary rejoice with the Carp—the ponds of Fairlawn and the garden bless for the master.

In the *Song*, the 24th stanza, in which it is said that David the supreme poet sang of fish, among his other subjects:

> The shoals upon the surface leap,
> And love the glancing sun—

also delves a way back into his experience, by way of a frequent image of metallic fish gliding through the water or breaking a still surface. In lines from the *Jubilate* already quoted, when he is returned from a punishment cell into the sunlight, he recalls the Bleak, those small, quick-gliding, quick-leaping, silver-bodied fish of English rivers, which cruise in shoals. There are such fish in *Hymn XIII* (which is closely linked to the *Jubilate* entries):

> Tansy, calaminth and daisies,
>   On the river's margin thrive;
> And accompany the mazes
>   Of the stream that leaps alive,

in the *Psalms* (No. CXLVII), in the fable *Munificence and Modesty;* and all of them occur far back in the childhood celebrations of Kent and the silver Medway which form so much of *The Hop-Garden.* Wood-nymphs in that early poem climb oaks over the river, and:

> in Medway's bosom fair
> Wonder at silver bleak, and prickly pearch,
> That swiftly thro' their floating forests glide.

The 52nd stanza of the *Song* offers one of the most fascinating crystallizations and intensifications of a thing seen:

> For ADORATION seasons change,
> And order, truth, and beauty range,
>   Adjust, attract and fill:
> The grass the polyanthus cheques;
> And polish'd porphyry reflects,
>   By the descending rill.

Anyone who knows, by good luck, the limestone country of Raby and of Staindrop Moor alongside (recalled by name in the *Jubilate* in 1759) and Teesdale will at once see the flower and the rock and the waterfall in a characteristic conjunction which Smart must have known in his Co. Durham days, the limestone so finely polished by centuries of the descending rill, protruding from grass chequered with the lilac umbels, by the thousand, of the Birdseye Primrose.[1]

More than a hundred lines in *A Song to David* can be directly referred to sensations from his reading or from nature which Smart had already recorded in other poems or in *Jubilate Agno*. The point is the way in which (for the most part) such sensations are transformed, as if he had been able to alter their molecular structure; indeed the way in which, or the degree to which, he also transformed his poetry in this climacteric poem. I am sure the suggestion that he came to something of a Berkeleyan view of nature and of perception is correct, and that it helps to explain the transformation. *Esse est percipi*: to be is to be perceived; intense perception is intense being. Certainly there are statements in the relevant fragments of *Jubilate Agno* which Smart may have derived from Berkeley's *Siris*, his *An Essay towards a New Theory of Vision*, or his *Treatise concerning the Principles of Human Knowledge;* the statements, for example, that 'nothing is so real as that which is spiritual', or that 'an IDEA is the mental vision of an object' (New Year, 1760). Ideas for Berkeley are things, 'the several combinations of sensible qualities which are called *things*'. Their reality in the mind, the abolition of the separation of the mind which perceives from the perceived, burnishes and enhances their existence. 'Ideas imprinted on the senses are real things, or do really exist' (*Principles*, Part I, 90). This notion of impression, of imprint, is a favourite one with Berkeley; and in *Jubilate* one discovers Smart proceeding from an idea, as a mental vision of an object, to take up exactly this printer's image of impression:

---

[1] Smart's frequently mentioned cowslips, gem-like:
> Cowslips, like topazes that shine,
> Muse by the silver serpentine

were rooted no doubt in the Kentish portion of his childhood, along with the gilt crucians, the silver bleak and silver roach. See *Epithalamium, Hymn XIII, The Blockhead and The Beehive*, and *Hymns for Children*, No. XXV.

For my talent is to give an impression upon words by punching,
that when the reader casts his eye upon 'em, he takes up the image
from the mould wch I have made.

As if nature, in all its width, produced its sense impressions
on him, which he in turn impressed upon words, which
in their turn transferred those impressions to the reader;
which is in fact what happens, as if a study of Berkeley
had been the refining and strengthening agent of his renewed
vision, helping him to avoid 'enthusiasm' (Berkeley ex-
pressly rejected the 'enthusiasm' of Malebranche—see the
second of the *Three Dialogues between Hylas and Philonous*),
to maintain his eighteenth century respect for reason, and
yet to give more freedom to the excited receptivity of his
senses. One has only to compare the slackness of Psalm CIV:

> And some of huge enormous bulk
> The swelling floods surmount

with the punch and the grand immediate perception of
the final:

> Strong against tide, the' enormous whale
> Emerges as he goes

in the 76th stanza of *A Song to David* or the original:

> Be thou my bulwark to defend
> Like some strong bastion's mole
> *Psalm XXXI*

with:

> Strong is the lion—like a coal
> His eyeball—like a bastion's mole
> His chest against the foes

in the same stanza; or the curt transmutation of:

> And let the multitudes in mail
> Before my God retire

(from Psalm LXVIII) into that unqualified verbless state-
ment and exclamation:

> Beauteous the multitudes in mail

of the 78th stanza, in order to appreciate the degree of
transformation or even transmutation. 'Impression' for
Smart was more than impression upon words. Introducing
his verse translation of Horace years later (1767) he wrote
in much the same way of 'the beauty, force, and vehemence
of *Impression*' as a 'talent or gift of almighty God, by
which a Genius is empowered to throw an emphasis on a
word or a sentence in such wise, that it cannot escape any
reader of sheer good sense, and true critical sagacity'. He
then talked of the 'impression' of qualities, melancholy,
strength, grandeur, sweetness, dignity, upon poetry; of
impression as the general characteristic of a poem: 'the
face of Impression is always liveliest upon the eulogies of
patriotism, gratitude' (cf. *A Song to David* as a thanksgiving
to David, whose own Psalms were 'the Book of Gratitude'),
'honour, and the like'. Impression shapes lines as well as
words in *A Song to David*, stanzas as well as lines, stanza-
groups as well as stanzas, and the whole as well as any part.
As usually printed, as printed by Smart himself, a cataract
of 86 stanzas thundering along without intermission to a
great finale, the poem seems at first haphazard, even con-
fused, without declaring its structure. The reader needs to
consult the analysis of the contents which Smart wrote as
an introduction, and then read it accordingly with breaks
or pauses between each proper group of stanzas. Smart's
analytical contents are not as clear as they might be; but
here are the divisions as he seems to have meant them and
made them:

> I—III: Invocation
> IV—XVII: The twelve Points of the excellence and lustre
> of David's Character
> XVIII—XXVI: The Subjects of his singing
> XXVII—XXIX: His victories won by song

It has been recognized that Smart hammered out the stanzas of the *Song* in groups and multiples of three and seven, the mystic numbers, with an occasional one, numbers which he approves in *Jubilate Agno*:

> For there is a mystery in numbers.
> For One is perfect and good being at unity in himself . . .
> For every thing infinitely perfect is Three . . .
> For Seven is very good consisting of two compleat numbers . . .
> For Nine is a number very good and harmonious,

the important thing being less the occult numeration or combination than the way in which the poem is impressed, again, with an intellectual structure, a harmony and proportion of parts which at once are parts and a whole. It is not a series of random images. In appropriate order, baroque detail, distance and immensity, near and far, small and large, still and active (consider, for instance, that fine stanza in which, close to, the silverlings and crusions glide, and far off, the 'pink and mottled vault' extends, in which there might be, though there isn't, an engagement of good and evil angels) are welded, impressed, into a coherent structure, with strong immediacy, strong verbs, strong inversions, strong rhymes, a strong rhythm (changing to tenderness when required); with those qualities, in short, of which Gerard Manley Hopkins spoke, when he felt their absence in his own verse, as roll and rise and carol and creation.

But this total 'impression', shaping and sustaining *A Song to David*, is also, like an 'idea' of Berkeley's, part of the language of the governing spirit, of God. It is 'a talent or gift of Almighty God', Smart had said in the wake of Berkeley; and in Berkeley's phrase it is the Author of Nature who imprints the ideas upon our senses:

> The phenomena of nature, which strike on the senses and are understood by the mind, form not only a magnificent spectacle, but also a most coherent, entertaining and instructive Discourse; and to effect this, they are conducted, and ranged by the greatest wisdom.
>
> (Berkeley, in *Siris*, section 254)

So here is the situation . . . A child is born, Christopher Smart, who has (like Traherne or the artist Samuel Palmer, or Gerard Manley Hopkins) the most receptive and open senses, the keenest ability, in his childhood in Kent, the Garden of England, and in Co. Durham, and later in his manhood, to perceive: perception, delight in perception, overlaid then renewed, finds religious warrant: religious warrant is subtilized and enforced (as with Traherne, Palmer, or Hopkins again) by philosophical speculation, till words, images, poems, (or at least one great poem) are at last informed with its wonderful degree of perception or load of reality. If the reader discounts the God, the degree of perception, the load of a wonderful reality, in a wonderful art, remains. If he reflects that wonder of perception can be induced by drugs, he should also admit that there can be difference of value. There is a difference between a God, or a physico-theology, in the mind, and a bottle of tablets on the hall table, or there would be to a theist, in his feeling about the effects of one or the other. *A Song to David* made a mixed impression on those who read it in 1763. 'A strange mixture of *dun obscure* and glowing genius at times' wrote Boswell to Samuel Johnson. 'I have seen his "Song to David" and from thence conclude him as mad as ever' wrote the correctly poised minor poet Mason to the correctly poised sentimental poet Gray, whose studies in natural history remained outside his evening or antiquarian verse. At the time when he had been taken ill again in 1759, Smart's friend and fellow denizen of Grub Street, Arthur Murphy, had come nearer the mark of his distinction: 'To hear thee', he wrote, when the *Song to David* had still to be conceived:

> Angels from their Golden Beds
> Willing bear down their Star-encircled Heads.

VII

A Song to David makes the strongest, most sustained use of Smart's peculiarity. In the *Hymns and Spiritual Songs*, in which he was again more free to invent than he had been in the *Psalms*, his praising also triumphs ecstatically, though rather in fragments, in a few stanzas in sequence or in single stanzas, than in whole poems. Hymn VI, *The Presentation of Christ in the Temple*, Hymn XIII, *St. Philip and St. James*, Hymn XIV, *The Ascension of Our Lord Jesus Christ*:

> They knew him well, and could not err,
>   To him they all appeal'd;
> The beast of sleek or shaggy fur,
> And found their natures to recur
>   To what they were in Eden's field.

> For all that dwell in depth or wave,
>   And ocean—every drop—
> Confess'd his mighty pow'r to save,
> When to the floods his peace he gave,
>   And bade careering whirlwinds stop.
>
> And all things meaner from the worm
>   Probationer to fly;
> To him that creeps his little term,
> And countless rising from the sperm
>   Shed by sea-reptiles, where they ply.
>
> These all were bless'd beneath his feet,
>   Approaching them so near . . .

also Hymn XXVIII, *All Saints*, and Hymn XXXII, *The Nativity of Our Lord and Saviour Jesus Christ*, are extraordinary outworks of praise, forceful and immediate in attack, in rhythm, in imagery and unexpectedness; but the reader is inclined to pick out his stanzas, and to break off, when the immediacy of impression becomes less. These poems lack the structural cohesion of the *Song*, which in one respect they curiously resemble. In the *Song*, passages of less imaginative force, stanzas XL to XLVIII particularly, are added, as if by afterthoughts of propriety, to the more compulsive grandeurs. This may be justified by effect, by giving the reader a pause, almost a rest, between the grandeurs. In the hymns, more and less compulsive parts are also joined, but unsuccessfully. For instance the *Nativity* hymn begins with five stanzas of rather ordinary writing, and suddenly changes to four stanzas of Smart's most compulsive and impressive felicity—

> Nature's decorations glisten
>   Far above their usual trim;
> Birds on box and laurels listen,
>   As so near the cherubs hymn.

Boreas now no longer winters
  On the desolated coast;
Oaks no more are riv'n in splinters
  By the whirlwind and his host.

Spinks and ouzles sing sublimely,
  'We too have a Saviour born',
Whiter blossoms burst untimely
  On the blest Mosaic thorn.

God all-bounteous, all-creative,
  Whom no ills from good dissuade,
Is incarnate, and a native
  Of the very world he made

as if these four stanzas alone were the ones 'given', the ones which compelled Smart and obsessed him in the making, and as if the five others had been a later intellectual contrivance. The poem falls in two. Smart was writing, after all, in confinement and derangement. To each *donnée* he may therefore have been all the more tempted to add stanzas of more ordinary exposition in proof to himself, if not to others, of his own sanity of coherence of mind. I suspect that, like the *Psalms*, the best of the *Hymns*, if not all of them, were written before the *Song to David*: the best ones read to me as if they had been in effect trial pieces, trial arrangements, which led him to the *Song* itself; the best portions of the best of the *Hymns* seem outcomes of that gathering pressure which at last moulded the *Song*.

What is one to say of the now celebrated *Jubilate Agno*, the manuscript of which survived by accident, and was not printed (and then in a misleading form) until 1939? That it is not a *poem*? So much is probably true. Smart cannot have thought of it as a poem, and I believe it is best looked at as a species of journal of its own kind, a day book journal of praise, which he recorded to begin with, antiphonally, in a Hebrew parallelism. Its value is more than biographical in the facts of biography and thought and in the revelation

of ebb and resurgence in Smart's illness of mind. Entries
such as:

> For black blooms and it is PURPLE

or,

> Let Ahimaaz rejoice with the Solver-Worm[1] who is a living
> mineral
> For there is silver in my mines and I bless God that it is rather
> there than in my coffers.

or,

> Let Hushim rejoice with the King's Fisher who is of royal beauty,
> tho' plebeian size
> For in my nature I quested for beauty, but God, God hath sent me
> to sea for pearls

(the last a most admirable and accurate description of himself as a poet) have shape and effect, and there are passages
enough of sharp lucidity, for instance, the celebrated
description of his cat Jeoffry, written in the summer of
1760, to counterbalance the many entries of peculiar praise
desperately or habitually maintained although derangement
or despondency of mind has reduced them to a formula.

VIII

After madness? To a summit, illness or no, one climbs,
A Song to David having been no miracle without roots or
prologue; from a summit, sanity or no, one descends. In
the asylum, in confinement on and off for seven years,
Smart was out of the world: whatever distress he felt, he
had been free of intellectual interference, he had been able
to dive for pearls in his own way. Fashions or habits of

---

[1] i.e. the Glow-worm.

mental (and literary) style were more against Smart in the seventeen-fifties than they had been, shall I say, against the equally well-educated Traherne in the previous century. Habits of correct and abstract elegance were against him, nor was he in tune with those strains of mood and melancholy which kept the effeminate, sentimental, literary and less 'real' poems of Gray, for example, popular for so long. Smart dealt in the immediate, the concrete, the thing sensed here and now, not in suffusions of mood yearning for the past, for the townsman's country, or anything else which is not there. Nearer the hard pearliness of the seventeenth century than the softer romanticism of the early nineteenth century, he recovered contact with his earlier habits of perception, he was able to recollect them fruitfully and to renew them, in a way which will be familiar to readers of the *Centuries* of Thomas Traherne.[1] Confinement helped him in this (much as it was to help John Clare) by isolating or insulating him. When he was restored to freedom in the early months of 1763, Smart was back in the world, and the world was at him again. He had climbed to a height of praise, a height of concrete passion, which could not be maintained; and the world fuddled and troubled him once more. There is a clear, uncommonly revealing, glimpse of Smart in October 1764, then aged 42, about a year and nine months after his release. He was busy. He had not returned to his wife and children, or his family. On his sister's behalf, the writer Hawkesworth called on him in cheerful rooms above Storey's Gate Coffee House, opening to a terrace which overlooked St. James's Park. He told Hawkesworth he was busy translating all of Horace into verse; Hawkesworth suggested he should go and see his sister in Kent. 'To this he replied very quick', and one can see him standing there and turning away his head, 'I cannot afford to be idle'; and within three years or so of

---

[1] For the probable course of Smart's development from perception to loss of it, and then its recovery, compare the first seven sections of Traherne's *Third Century*.

his release he busily published *A Song to David*, two small collections of verse, an oratorio, *Hannah* (which was sung at the King's Theatre in the Haymarket), a verse translation of Phaedrus, and his *Psalms and Hymns*, for which he had at last rounded up enough subscribers.

The new poems included two odes, written just before his release, one to an admiral, one to a general, each of whom had recently been victorious in action. (Smart—like John Clare—has a small man's admiration for military prowess.) They exhibit his peculiar concrete eloquence, especially the *Ode to General Draper:*

> What tho' no bonfires be display'd,
>   Nor windows light up the nocturnal scene;
> What tho' the merry ringer is not paid,
>   Nor rockets shoot upon the STILL SERENE;
> Tho' no matross upon the rampart runs,
> To send out thy report from loud redoubling guns? . . .

The poems in his miscellaneous collection of 1763 included also a fable, *Reason and Imagination*, which Smart published so soon after his release as if to assert his restored rationality. Imagination, Queen of Imagery, proposes marriage to Reason, that proper 'Attribute of Man' who is 'solid, weighty, deep, and sound,' and offers to elevate him from his hole and ditch 'To gay Conception's top-most pitch'. Reason declines, and proposes to be an ally and nothing else:

> I cannot take thee for a mate;
> I'm lost, if e'er I change my state.
> But whensoe'er your raptures rise,
> I'll try to come with my supplies
> But, ere this treaty be agreed
> Give me thy wand and winged steed:
> Take thou this compass and this rule,
> That wit may cease to play the fool;
> And that thy vot'ries who are born
> For Praise, may never sink to scorn.

James Boswell thought the fable 'very pretty', and saw in the other poems 'shivers of genius' here and there, though they were 'often ludicrously low'. Such shivers recur in the poems Smart had still to write. His translations of Horace—all of Horace—which came out in four volumes in 1767, swing from the shivers to the low, and back again, after the introduction, edgy and slightly eccentric, in which he expounds his too brief views about 'impression'. If at times ridiculous, clumsy or careless, his translation can be very direct in style:

> I hate the mob , and drive them hence,
> Lost to all sanctity and sense . . .

It can be affecting:

> Ah! Postumus, the years, the years,
> Glide swiftly on, nor can our tears
> Or piety the wrinkl'd age forefend,
> Or for one hour retard th' inevitable end . . .

It can be gay and lyrical:

> Pyrrha, for whom with such an air
> Do you bind back your golden hair?

It can be entirely surprising in its change of rhythm and manner, for instance in Smart's version of Book I, Ode XXXVIII, to Horace's servant:

> Persian's pomps, boy, ever I renounce them:
> Scoff o' the plaited coronet's refulgence;
> Seek not in fruitless vigilance the rose-trees
>   Tardier offspring.
>
> Mere honest myrtle that alone is order'd,
> Me the mere myrtle decorates, as also
> Thee the prompt waiter to a jolly toper
>   Hous'd in an arbour.

These translations were once unfairly neglected, they are now extravagantly proclaimed; which at least is better. Smart's lifelong forte, though, was praise; it was praise, not translation—even of David's psalms—which called out his full power of impression; and, as if in defence of short-comings, he remarks, in his introduction to the Horace, that 'there is a little-ness in the noblest poet among the Heathens when compared to the prodigious grandeur and genuine majesty of a *David* or *Isaiah*'.

In verse and in life from now on there are only a few more glimpses of Smart. One or two concrete and affecting scraps illuminate the somewhat exhausted simplicity of his last effort of praise, *Hymns for the Amusement of Children* who could hardly have found amusement among the rest in the 24th Hymn, *Melancholy*, in which he asks:

> How to begin, and how to depart,
>   From this sad fav'rite theme,
> The man of sorrow in my heart,
> I at my own ideas start,
>   As dread as Daniel's dream.

Two years earlier he had written pathetically personal and unmannered songs in his second oratorio, *Abimelech* (1768), the one which begins:

> There is no rose to minds in grief;
>   There is no lilly for despair;
> Tears and distraction are relief,
>   And yews and willows we must wear,

and better still, the three stanzas which look back to his earliest life at Fairlawn:

> Ah, memory, my cruel foe,
> How much you daily work for woe!
>   The past upon the present hour,
> How I was miss'd you bring to view,
> And all my former scenes renew,
>   My ev'ning walks, my fav'rite bow'r.

The friendship I was wont to share,
The flow'rs I nursed with so much care;
   My garden, grotto, and my bees,
And, all those little griefs above,
My mother's and my sister's love,
   And father's blessing on my knees.

Yet taunter of the past delight,
That urgest grief in such despight,
   Some soothing pow'rs to thee belong:
Do not those soothing pow'rs refuse,
But, as the mother of the Muse,
   Shape all my sorrows into song.

He is to be seen a few times through the eye of the young sixteen year old and seventeen year old Fanny Burney. He comes to call on her father, his old friend the musician, Dr. Burney. 'He is extremely grave', she says in 1768, 'and has still great wildness in his manner, looks, and voice.' He comes a year later in flowerless autumn: 'Poor Mr. Smart presented me this morning with a rose, blooming and sweet as if we were in the month of June. "It was given me", said he "by a fair lady—though not so fair as *you*." ' From his debtor's prison, to which he was committed in 1771, so fulfilling all of Thomas Gray's early prediction, he writes to Burney, asking him to help a prisoner worse off than himself, and saying that he had himself 'already assisted [him] according to my willing poverty'. It was in prison that he died, not long after his forty-ninth birthday, on 21 May, 1771. But these last glimpses present Christopher Smart in the wrong character of pathos. His existence is in the hard immediate exultancy of his truest verse, above all in *A Song to David*, in which, in Coleridge's phrase, he is a bridler by delight, a purifier, contriving a firmness out of the chaotic.

CHRISTOPHER SMART

A Select Bibliography

(Place of publication London, unless stated otherwise)

Bibliography:

'A BIBLIOGRAPHY OF THE WRITINGS' by G. J. Gray (1902)

—in *Transactions of the Bibliographical Society*, VI.

Collected Works:

POEMS, 2 vols. Reading (1791)

—omits 'A Song of David' and other poems; but includes a biographical sketch by the poet's nephew, Christopher Hunter.

COLLECTED POEMS, edited by N. C. Callan, 2 vols. (1949)

—in the Muses' Library. Omits some of the translations and oratorios, and the Latin poems.

POEMS, edited by R. E. Brittain, Princeton (1950)

—a selection only, but the best critical edition, with notes, and items from the *Horace*, *Hannah* and *Abimelech*.

Separate Works:

THE HORATIAN CANONS OF FRIENDSHIP (1750)

—'The Third Satire of the first Book of Horace Imitated.'

ON THE ETERNITY OF THE SUPREME BEING. Cambridge (1750)

—the Seatonian Prize Poem, 1750.

AN OCCASIONAL PROLOGUE AND EPILOGUE TO OTHELLO (1751)

A SOLEMN DIRGE, SACRED TO THE MEMORY OF FREDERICK, PRINCE OF WALES (1751)

THE NUT CRACKER. CONTAINING AN AGREEABLE VARIETY OF WELL SEASONED JESTS &c. (1751)

ON THE IMMENSITY OF THE SUPREME BEING. Cambridge (1751)

—the Seatonian Prize Poem, 1751.

AN INDEX TO MANKIND: OR MAXIMS SELECTED FROM THE WITS OF ALL NATIONS (1751)

POEMS ON SEVERAL OCCASIONS (1752)

ON THE OMNISCIENCE OF THE SUPREME BEING. Cambridge (1752)

—the Seatonian Prize Poem, 1752.

THE HILLIAD: AN EPIC POEM (1753)

—only 'Book I' was published of this satire, occasioned by a feeble literary quarrel.

ON THE POWER OF THE SUPREME BEING. Cambridge (1754)
—the Seatonian Prize Poem, 1754.

ON THE GOODNESS OF THE SUPREME BEING. Cambridge (1756)
—the Seatonian Prize Poem, 1756.

HYMN TO THE SUPREME BEING ON RECOVERY FROM A DANGEROUS FIT OF
ILLNESS (1756)

THE WORKS OF HORACE, TRANSLATED LITERALLY INTO ENGLISH PROSE.
2 vols. (1756)
—reprinted in Bohn's Classical Library, 1850, and in part (the Satires
and Epistles) in Everyman's Library, 1911.

THE NONPAREIL: OR, THE QUINTESSENCE OF WIT AND HUMOUR (1757)
—an anthology of Smart's contributions to *The Midwife, or the Old
Woman's Magazine*, 1750–53.

MRS. MIDNIGHT'S ORATIONS: AND OTHER SELECT PIECES (1763)

A SONG TO DAVID (1763)
—type facsimile, 1926. The editions by E. Blunden, 1924, and P.
Serale, 1924, and the limited edition by J. B. Broadbent, 1960, are
valuable. The fullest commentary is in *English Prose and Poetry*,
1680–1800, edited by O. Shepard and P. S. Wood, Boston, 1934.

POEMS, VIZ. REASON AND IMAGINATION, A FABLE [1763]
—with three other pieces.

POEMS ON SEVERAL OCCASIONS, VIZ. MUNIFICENCE AND MODESTY [1763]
—with eight other pieces.

HANNAH: AN ORATORIO [1764]

ODE TO THE RIGHT HONOURABLE THE EARL OF NORTHUMBERLAND . . .
WITH SOME OTHER PIECES (1764)

A POETICAL TRANSLATION OF THE FABLES OF PHAEDRUS (1765)
—reprinted in Bohn's Classical Library, 1853.

THE WORKS OF HORACE TRANSLATED INTO VERSE, 4 vols. (1767)

A TRANSLATION OF THE PSALMS OF DAVID (1768)
—includes *A Song of David*.

ABIMELECH. AN ORATORIO [1768]

THE PARABLES OF OUR LORD AND SAVIOUR JESUS CHRIST. DONE INTO
FAMILIAR VERSE FOR THE USE OF YOUNGER MINDS (1768)

HYMNS FOR THE AMUSEMENT OF CHILDREN (3rd edition 1775)
—no earlier edition is known. A facsimile of this edition was published
by the Luttrell Society in 1947.

PROVIDENCE: AN ORATORIO (1777)
—the recitatives excerpted from Smart's Seatonian Prize Poems.

REJOICE IN THE LAMB, edited by W. F. Stead (1939)
—the first publication of *Jubilate Agno*.
JUBILATE AGNO, edited by W. H. Bond. Harvard (1954)
—the standard text, re-arranged according to the sequence of the
    original MS.

Some Critical and Biographical Studies:

PARLEYING WITH CERTAIN PEOPLE OF IMPORTANCE IN THEIR DAY, by
    R. Browning (1887)
—one section is given to Smart, and Browning's interest helped in
    Smart's rediscovery during the nineteenth century.
DISCOVERIES, by J. M. Murry (1924)
CHRISTOPHER SMART, SA VIE ET SES OEUVRES, par K. A. McKenzie.
    Paris (1925)
'Christopher Smart's Madness', by C. D. Abbott (1930)
—in *PMLA*, XLV.
STUDII BRITANNICI, by F. Olivero. Turin (1931)
—contains a valuable study of *A Song to David*.
THE CASE OF CHRISTOPHER SMART, by L. Binyon (1934)
—English Association: Pamphlet No. 90.
'The Structure of Smart's *Song to David*', by R. D. Havens (1938)
—in *Review of English Studies*, XIV.
SMART: A BIOGRAPHICAL AND CRITICAL STUDY, by E. G. Ainsworth and
    C. E. Noyes. Columbia, Missouri (1943)
—in *University of Missouri Studies*, XVIII, 4.
'Smart, Berkeley, the Scientists and the Poets', by D. J. Greene (1953)
—in *Journal of the History of Ideas*, XIV.
'The probable time of the Composition of Christopher Smart's *Song
    to David*, *Psalms*, and *Hymns and Songs*', by A. Sherbo (1956)
—in *Journal of English and Germanic Philology*, LV.
POOR KIT SMART, by C. Devlin (1961)